Analog Poems

Matthew Wood

Copyright © 2016 Matthew Wood

ALL RIGHTS RESERVED. This book contains material protected under International and Federal Copyright Laws and Treaties. Any unauthorized reprint or use of this material is prohibited. No part of this book may be reproduced or transmitted in any form or by any means, electronic or mechanical, including photocopying, recording, or by any information storage and retrieval system without express written permission from the author/publisher.

ISBN: 978-1-944878-03-0

For Norah

Contents

Poetry 1

My Students 2

The Big Three 3

(What Could Be) The Biggest Lies 4

The Life You Write May Be Your Own 5

Work in Progress 7

Thought Too Much/Draught Too Much 8

A Poem To No One/A Poem To Someone 9

For All I Know 10

Long Division 11

Friendly Fire 13

Really Real 14

I'm (Not) That Type of Guy 15

First World Savagery 16

A Little Truth (This Is Not a Love Poem) 18

To All The Hipsters 21

Alphabet Enlightenment 23

I Want To Know 24

Easier To Be Green 26

Thunder Storms and Thoughts on Changing Opinions
    Regarding Said Storms Sparked by a Beautiful Muse 27

Mental Health Status, Part One: Alcohol 29

Mental Health Status, Part Two: Anxiety..30

Mental Health Status, Part Three: Identity 31

At the Bar..34

Meghan..36

Going Home (November 3, 2012) 38

Wordfare 41

Race Day (Hopeless Romantic or Romantic Hopeless)....................43

Hip Hop (In The Name of Love)...44

Waking Up..45

Acknowledgments

To my family both blood and extended (please don't kill me if your name isn't here, y'all know who you are) for always pushing me to this point. Ma and Pa, Buzz and Linda, Cris, Patrick and Jennifer, Chad, Russ, Shelby (without a doubt in my heart, but also for helping me find the logistical way to do this), S.K.P. (your belief in me is no small thing), to the poets and lyricists and writers that have and continue to inspire me too numerous to list, Chris and Debbie at JETLAUNCH, my Kickstarter backers (keep looking through the collection, there's a page JUST for you!), and God for helping me find the pens and notebooks.

Poetry

I'll keep spitting poetry
Spitting poetry because life shows no symmetry
No balance to hold for stability
Realized I have to make my own gravity
Been knocked down
Dragged down
Shots kept coming even when I was on the ground
No time to make my face frown
No choice I have to get back up
I haven't lived life or given enough
There's a catch, a snag, struggle
Being bulletproof comes with a price
Stings like hell though spared my life
That's what I take
Take, take, take
For what or who's sake?
I don't know
On I go
Shots fired and I take them
No choice about it, no chance to run
Not even sure who's hand holds that gun
No matter what, I'll live
I've got a love and a life to give.
I'm spitting poetry
Spitting poetry to make my own symmetry
My own stability
My own gravity
Spitting poetry

My Students

Every morning I come through the B hallway door.
Not sure what or who will challenge me.
Strolling along. saying, "hey." Hoping my belongings don't drop to the floor,
Seeing students seeing me fumbling for my keys.

First period is a trip, truly is.
I am far more awake than any of these kids.
Inevitably, one or two of them will jump head first into a dis,
But basically, it's up to me to help them avoid these kinds of skids.

The game I play is all about turning on the lights,
Turning on tunes, planning plus improv equals learning.
Showing them what they know, but think is beyond their sights,
I'm trying to turn trudges and tribulations into yearning.

I see it, tomorrow is not just a new day,
It is a view into doing this a brand new way.

The Big Three

My own personal saints,
I've got three.
They say everything always comes in comes threes.
First is Saint Christopher,
For my soul's travels,
My "shotgun" saint on the peddle to the metal.
What do you say Chris? Want to see what she can do?
Saint number two: Anthony.
For those times I'm lost,
Without a map,
Up Shit's Creek without a paddle.
Last, but not least: Isabelle.
My model of peace and charity,
To remind me, that no matter what,
Even when life knocks my teeth out,
That the world is much bigger than me,
And that everyone is in the fight of their lives.

(What Could Be) The Biggest Lies

So hard to try, so easy to say.
Thinking hurts a little.
Sometimes, all it does is hurt.
So I write this poem that borders on whiny,
Bumps that line of emo.

I hate that shit.

Truth of it is, these are the thoughts that I should think.
Thoughts that should see light
That should see action
That should be said
Thoughts that are faster than they ever look
Stronger than they appear
These thoughts look so daunting, so immense.

Here's another truth about these thoughts -
To keep them is wrong, damn near unlawful.
Never to try them is to never see them,
Creating more what ifs than bearable.

Keeping these thoughts becomes more than painful.
Honestly, sincerely, what it really does is this -
Keeping any of them becomes the biggest lies never told.

The Life You Write May Be Your Own

A long time ago I realized that I should keep writing,
and I should write like my life depends on it.
For the life I write may be my own.
Every syllable, word, comma, period,
apostrophe, pulls it all together,
strings every heartbeat, breath, minute,
day, and beyond, into one continuous life.
A life that lives to learn.
A life that has only just begun to figure out how to just be.

I write like my life depends on it.
Like every word might be my last.
Like each word is more vital than the last.
This life I write just may be my own.
So I scrutinize every word to the letter,
every tense to make sure I live in the present,
a present to unwrap like every day is Christmas,
a gift like every day is my birthday.
I'm that kid wiping the sleep from my eyes. I'm awake.

To everyone I meet, write like your life depends on it.
Treat every word like they are the building blocks to your own Constitution.
Use every word like it's your personal Declaration of Independence,
all of it, because the life you write may be your own.
Know that what you say and how you say it can make you a force that has
never before been seen.
Know that even the "unmovable" can be budged, and pushed,
that the word "unbreakable" is just a front. Discover that in your words.
Your words. Fight with them, write with them, write them down,
because the life that you write just may be your own.

For Bianka

Work in Progress

He is a good guy,
Somewhere between Jesus Christ and John Lennon.
Living righteously, as much as he can anyway,
Though there is always Saturday night.
But it's Saturday that makes the work for Sunday.
A good guy, really, I mean, really he is.
A heart like the Grinch's,
After he heard the Who's singing without the presents and fixings,
After he carved the roast beast.
Reaching out to pull people closer,
To protect,
To share the sanctity of love.
Oh the backslide!
Backsliding is the fun of it!
Like I said, got to have something to do come Sunday.
In the end, He will judge him,
He will say, "Come on up, kick back,
Beer is in the fridge."
See, I'm telling you,
He's a good guy, really, somewhere between Jesus Christ and John Lennon.

Thought Too Much/Draught Too Much

I know I might drink too much
Been said I do
Think too much
Been said I do
Drink so I don't have to think too much
But I still think a lot
Even when I drink a lot,
So I keep on with the drink a lot
Because why the fuck not?
I function
I fit
I do what I'm supposed to
I do my shit
So I keep drinking
To slow my thinking
But every drink, I fucking swear,
Makes me do more of the think
And so that cycle rolls on
And on
And on
And
On
Thinking to drinking to more thinking
To
More
Drinking
I see no stopping either
I see no legitimate reason
I'm feeling what I'm supposed to be feeling
Dealing how I'm supposed to be dealing
So I come around again
Nothing to lose
Nothing to win
I'm going to keep thinking too much
Side by side with drinking too much

A Poem To No One/A Poem To Someone

I can feel that you're a good soul,
and all I want is to get to know you better.
I don't really know what that means just yet,
But I know that I mean it.
I also know that my heart jumps like a giddy kid on his birthday when you're around.
When I see you.
When I think of you.
I know that there's an excitement,
That rush of meeting someone.
Someone new that you can't wait to see again.
To talk to again.
How incredibly great, exhilarating,
Insanely beautiful would it be if...
If every day from here felt exactly this way?
That every thought, word, look, would be just like this?
Just as electric and exciting all the time?
And why can't it be?
Or shouldn't it be?
Dammit, it really can be.

For All I Know

What?
Of course I want to talk.
Yeah, I know it's 2am, but you got me up. Let's do this!
Here's the thing though,
Why wouldn't you want to talk?
I'm going to tell you right now,
I see the pressure on you.
I feel it when you walk into the room.
That push to be everything to everyone.
I see what you're eating to prove it,
Or, I should say, what you don't eat.
Like Napoleon said to Debbie about the milk, "you could drink the 2%."
I see you putting on another face,
Who the hell told you the one you were born with isn't beautiful?
Because it is.
The simple fact is, guys should be killing for you.
Slaying dragons and monsters.
Laying them to rest.
So you can rest.
So that when 2am comes,
You're already in Dreamland,
And you've been there for hours.

Long Division

There's something fuzzy about your math.
I'm not sure if it all adds up right.
Subtracts the same though.
But like some long division problem,
Remainders are everywhere,
Finding the lowest common denominators,
I just don't know.
Logic has always had an elusive quality.
Escapes me on the best of days.
Abstractions have even looser connections
Sitting somewhere between absolutes and obscurities.
My head hurts.
My heart isn't that far behind.

Friendly Fire

Wording is close to everything,
Searching for what I mean, what I want,
Some feel like shots fired.
Though it's friendly fire,
Friendly fire.
The kind coming from allied forces.
Coming from where no one should expect it.
(Is that why it hurts more?)
Looking enemies straight in the eyes
To get hit from behind
Friendly fire.
The kind that doesn't come from enemy lines
The kind that makes the cliché so true
The one that's on that "it's not you, it's me" thing
The one that says "it's not something you did or didn't do"
Friendly fire
The kind no one should expect.
But the kind that happens too much.

Really Real

Reality is just a word.
Apparently it depends on who uses it.
Whatever it means to one, pulls the other down.
So what happens if it's not real?
What happens when promises are just sounds?
Sounds and syllables?
Not words and meanings?
When they're just a random string of audio?
Said for melody and flow?
That must make the breaks harmless.
The betrayals just a change of space and scenery.
The hurt is make believe.
The products of sheer will and imagination.
Conglomerates of "what ifs" and hypotheticals.
Of "what would you do's?"
What this is though is a big, "what does it matter?"
An even larger, "it really doesn't."
"Shouldn't."
But it does.
It is real. Way too much so.
It's all real.
Real as real gets, painful as hurt is.
Though on the other side, it never counted.
Even with obvious effects.
A total of what the pieces were together,
Last was always where it all finished.
Where I placed.

I'm (Not) That Type of Guy

From the very bottom of my broken...
No. Forget that noise.
I'm not that type of guy.
I'm this type of guy...
I talk about where I'm from and what I've been through with pride.
A pride that I've lived through what I have and still stand.
I'm not the type of guy that will fight you,
Throw down with you,
Hurt and hit you.
I'm the type that will protect the ones I love.
I'm the type that won't stop till you do.
I'm not the rip you limb for limb type,
I'm the type that knows what scrappy means.
What else?
I'm the type of guy that worries.
Worries about what you'll eat for dinner because you ruined it.
Because you ruined it in anger at me for not wanting to be shit on,
Ruining what I thought would be a quiet night.
Yeah, I'm not that type of guy.
The type that won't worry,
That will stop caring.
I'm the type of guy that tries,
With everything I've got,
To be bigger, stronger.
Am I the type of guy that can be someone's "only?"
Someone's "other" of significance?
I don't know.
I'm the type of guy that tries,
But still hasn't figured that out yet.
I'm the type of guy that doesn't want to hurt anyone,
But, whether I mean to or not, I know I will.
I'm the type of guy that will work like hell to make amends though.
I'm not the type of guy that knows all the answers.
I'm not the type of guy that will let that stop me.
I'm the type of guy that doesn't give up.
I'm the type of guy that can get hit hard to the ground,
Get back up with a shit eating grin that says, "that all you got?"
Because I'm not the type of guy who's that easy.

First World Savagery

There are a bunch of savages in this world.
Living on the blood of others.
Savagery.
They say
That is, it's in the text books,
Historians state that not a single shot was fired during the Cold War.
The millions burned in Hiroshima and Nagasaki may have a different opinion on that.
Not a single shot, but two very big bombs.
Brutality against humanity doesn't get a pass on the so called laurels of technological advance.
First world savagery.
Back in the day, or a few days ago maybe
The southern trees had the most morbid of decorations.
Billie sang a song about some strange fruit
People given life sentences for the crime of not being white.
Slavery ended, a poison purged, but there was more.
First world savagery.
A boy with a life in front of him gets pulled from a night out so motherfuckers with some insecurities can show him that they don't like that he likes boys.
Leave him for dead in a place that can only be considered nowhere.
First world savagery.
There are children, right now, trying to sleep on stomachs so empty that "hungry" doesn't even begin say what's what.
They will probably die before I finish this poem.
We let them starve because we say their parents are lazy.
First world savagery.
This is just the smallest of nutshells. We live in this world.
This sheltered little glass house.
We're Americans god dammit!
You can't touch this!
Oh wait!
Looks like you can...
April 19, 1995
Wait!
September 11, 2001
Wait!

April 15, 2013
Wait!
The list is long...
But hold up!
This is America motherfuckers, that's not allowed!
Stop this train now...
This is first world savagery.
And you've condoned it.
No more of this blame game on the minority for the insecurities and ignorance of the shit you spill in the name of patriotism, and fuck, really!? In the name of God?
Fuck you with that!
If you are the patriot and the Christian you claim you are, you'll realize that you've been commanded to never let Matthew die.
To never let a southern tree bare strange fruit.
To never let Diallo get shot even once... Let alone 41 times.
To never let millions die in an unforgettable fire.
Drones don't make this shit any better.
Otherwise, go get more tea, have a party for all I care.
But, admit this;
You are a first world savage.
Committing and condoning first world savagery.

A Little Truth (This Is Not a Love Poem)

This is not a love poem.
This is a truth poem.
This is a poem about how I think.
How I feel.
How I am.
This is a truth poem about it all.
The truth about how when we started talking I wasn't looking for anything.
Not anything heavy.
Not anything like... you know?
A relationship.
Friendship absolutely.
When you get along you get along.
But the rest?
Well you know?
Then a funny thing happened.
I got excited about talking to you.
Even more about seeing you.
Every time I'd get either my heart would...
Wait, no.
I mean to say that the stars...
No.
What I'm trying to say is birds sing...
No. Fuck the flowery poetics!
What I really mean to say is this:
I fucking love you.
That the truth of this poem,
The truth behind all compliments,
The fact that what I say only puts to words what is there.
It's not just how I see you.
It's you.
This still isn't a love poem.
It's a truth poem.
A truth poem about impact.
The truth of two people.
Affect, affection, cause and effect.
That sometimes life does throw a break.
That collisions aren't always damaging.
The truth that I know what I've got now.

What I'm capable of.
The truth of what you are.
Not just to me, but what you really are.
For all of it, in no small way.
I love you.
And that,
That.
That is the truth.
This is the truth.
This is still not a love poem.

To All The Hipsters

How many hipsters does it take to screw in a light bulb?
"Some obscure number you've probably never heard of."
How many hipsters?
"I can tell you, but just know that I knew the answer first."
How many hipsters?
Hold up.
You know what? There's a problem here.
A problem with this idea,
This mentality,
This way it has become *in* to discover something and keep it locked away.
Wrapped up like it's better left a secret.
Touting it like it's some kind of pop culture elitism.
Or worse.
Giving someone a supposed reason to put down.
To look down at others.
Just because person A might not have heard of something person B has.
No.
When did it become cool to do this?
What happened to those moments when a person finds something so great it just has to be talked about and shared without question?
Shared in the company of others with unbridled enthusiasm?
What happened?
Instead, you hipsters try to keep it all to yourselves.
As if it's some sort of badge of honor?
Another feather in your cap?
But, hey hipster, do you know what it really is?
It's another mark of asshole-ism.
Another exhibit of how much of a snob you really are.
So, I've got a simple challenge for you. For me. For all of us,
If you find something that charges you up
Moves you
Gives you goose bumps
Shakes you
Makes an impact on you
Affects you
Share it!
For fuck's sake, share it.
Make it a reason to bring people together.

Rather than fueling the fires of isolation let's celebrate that album
that movie
that painting
Maybe even this poem.
Celebrate these things with others.
So fuck the "bah humbugs" and Scrooging,
If it's charging you up
Moving you
Goose bumping you
Shaking you
Or who knows? Inspiring you.
Tell another soul about it.
And let's get together for it!

Alphabet Enlightenment

Activate my attention, my aural plane.
Be the beat in my brain, banging that bass drum.
Catch the cascade, cool my canopy.
Deal the downbeat on a dime, don't dare stop.
Everything is everything, everlasting when I emotionally connect. Electric.
Fantastical, further than free, footing not the final figure.
Greatness only given when the good gets going, going keeps growing.
Heavens, hells, heroes, heals. Hello to it all, hoping for a clear difference between halos and horns.
Intelligence for strength internal, independence, Iconic identification.
Jumping on the wings of joy. Joining the joy, jockeying for forever. Jubilation.
Kindness is my religion, killing that hate that Klans live in. Kinetic flow.
Letting loss live again as lessons for living, for loving.
Mountains can be moved, maneuvered, made massive, made miniature, my mood makes and breaks them.
Never give up; never give in, not for negative. No one. Never. Not once.
Operate on other planes, optimism can obliterate oppression.
Power is found in peace, punctuation, paragraphs, poems.
Quandaries, questions, quizzes, quests, never stop questioning.
Rest when revelry is reached. Rocky roads won't rope me down.
Still, never stop the surge that strikes, sustenance for my soul.
Timid, trepidation, torrential, traffic. Terms that tempt the topple of my temple.
Understanding, uncompromising, unwavering, unstoppable.
Vital signs vivaciously making new vectors. Venting vexations.
Wandering to start wondering, wondering to welcome words.
X-ray visions creating extraordinary spirit that can't be found at Xavier.
Yours is your world. You, for you. Yourself alone. You.
Zenith, one day, the Zenith.

I Want To Know

I want to know so many things
I want to know why the universe exploded
And why the stars continue to shine
I want to know why Jay walking is a crime
I want to know
I want to know how to calculate complex mathematical problems
I want to know why algebra really does matter
But do you want me to tell you what I really want to know?
I want to know your voice
And all of your different tones that come with all of your different emotions
I want to know your eyes and all of the ways they see those same emotions
I want to know how it feels to have your head on my shoulder
And how your hair smells when you do
I want to know what it feels like to have your fingers locked in between mine
Mine locked in yours
I want to know what you worry about
So I can be behind you through it all
I want to know what your hopes and dreams are
So I can cheer you on as you reach for them and grab them
I even want to know what your face looks like when I make you mad
So I can know how good it feels to see your face when I make it up to you and you forgive me
Do you want to know what I want to know?
It's you
I want to know you

Easier To Be Green

As a kid, I had more ear infections than I could count.
To the point I drank more antibiotics than water.
At the least, I was at Boston Eye and Ear monthly.
New tubes, another earplug fitting, yet another procedure.
From the house, to the T, to the specialists.
Not how I wanted to miss school,
I never played sick, my ears made sure of that.
It was such a routine.
Until one day -

I lived with The Muppets, I lived on the street,
Sesame Street.
Do you know how to get there?
You should.

There was this one day,
Routine as all the other visits to eye and ear were,
I'm put under for new tubes, I still hate the smell and taste of that gas.
I awake and the first face I see is green.
Kermit is waiting for me.
Ping pong ball eyes and green felt body and all.
From that day on there would be no hurdle too tall,
Kermit was there.
All other ear procedures, right there with me.
Kermit lived for the road too.
He was my road trip buddy.
From Dorchester to the Green Mountains, and back to Dorchester,
Always right there, ready for the ride.

As a kid I faced more tests than I could count.
Kermit was my shield.
My partner in crime,
My space ship co-pilot.
The galaxies we'd reach so far, far away.
A long way from Samoset Street.
A long way from Sesame Street.
But, always a shortcut to the heart of my childhood,
To the heart of me.
Thank you Kermit, for making it easier to be green.

Thunder Storms and Thoughts on Changing Opinions Regarding Said Storms Sparked by a Beautiful Muse

When I was a little I was deathly afraid.
Thunder storms spelled certain doom.
Like an impending dentist appointment,
Dark skies made me tense.
Slightest of rumbles sent me into hiding.
I was a fugitive.
It didn't matter how far away the sound was
That rumble meant that I was on the run to home
Or if I couldn't get there...
If I couldn't get there I lost my mind.
I resorted to locking myself in ma's car too.
So I never stuck around to see the lights.
These fears, they're sort of like tastes though
As you go, they might change
At some point in time, it's worth trying again
I don't know when it happened, but it did.
What stayed is that child like look out.
Finding that fear and awe run with each other.
Right?
Then there was this one summer,
Literally the most electric summer I can remember.
If I said every day was accented with lightning,
I wouldn't be exaggerating.
Not much anyway.
But, that summer...
Seeing lightning strike more times than countable.
Hearing that sound it makes.
Explosions.
Exploding.
The current's sonic signature.
Seeing something so fast the mere glimpse of it is on its way home,
The crash and boom like a thief that announces his presence to say,
"I'm here, now I'm gone, and there's not a damn thing you can do about it."
Just awesome,
To the roots of that word
It's all there, lightning and thunder make awe.
In that awe I feel small.

I feel small in all great ways.
Small for every right reason I can muster.
Beyond the science of ozone gasses and electricity,
I've come to see thunder storms as a path to be humble.
As a way to find humility.
The surgical precision of a single bolt.
The reaching grip of finger like chains.
As some look like veins carrying blood.
All beautiful.
All coming with massive strength.
Culminating in what beauty really is:
A marriage of grace and raw power.
With time, my view of thunder storms has changed.
From fear, admiration is born.
And I'm star struck every time I see one.
The view goes…
Fear makes admiration,
Admiration makes respect,
Respect makes fear.
All taking the form of lightning itself.
Strokes and return strokes.
Electric currents to remind me to be human.

for Meghan

Mental Health Status, Part One: Alcohol

How We Get Along

I'm not sleeping right.
I'm not eating right.
I'm drinking.
No, I'm not missing a word.
That was intentional.
As intentional as every sip of every drink that has crossed my lips.
Do I have demons? I do.
I drink my demons and 99% of the time I enjoy every, single, fucking drop.
All of them. In bottles, cans, glasses and by the occasional shot.
All of them.
Do I want to stop?
I have a few jokes lined up for why I don't.
And there's a truth in every joke.
So that's what's up.
Thanks for asking.
Me and my demons are getting along just fine.

Mental Health Status, Part Two: Anxiety

Everyday Anxious

"How are you?"
"I'm good. You?"
"Good."
That's how we all want it to go.
So we can move through a day without issue.
Or quote unquote, DRAMA.
Without acknowledging the stress we all know is there.
At some point, that elephant might get the hint and just go away.
Right?
No one wants a real answer to those questions.
No one.
No one wants me to answer the, "how are you?" with what's really up.
"Hi, how are you?"
"Ah, you know? I'm exhausted. I've been working a lot. Drinking more. Sleeping like shit. And when I do finally sleep I'm shaken awake by a fucked up dream or anxiety. Or both. And when I'm awake for the day, I can't stop moving. When I do stop moving, I shake. A lot. With or without caffeine. On the brink of tears at minimum. Though most likely there's an anxiety attack right around the corner. So yeah, I'm good."
That answer will always get one of a few responses.
Most often a "there there" or a "chin up buddy!"
Or worse, the other person turns it into a bad day pissing contest.
No matter what.
All dismissive.
All denial.
All blowing past the idea that if I, or anyone, actually answered like that.
With the truth of how I really feel in my day to day.
It would be an obvious need to legitimately cry for help.
That I'm struggling to even just. Get. By.
So it comes back to this:
"Hi! How are you!?"
"I'm fine! Thanks for asking!"

Mental Health Status, Part Three: Identity

Me Vs. Matt

I am everything everyone says I am
Kind, good, funny, giving, laid back, calm, closed off, walled,
emotionally unavailable, an asshole.
At one point I was trying to figure this out
Trying to find out which parts of that list are true.
Fact, I'm all of those things.
And then some.
Trouble is people so often see what they want.
They see this goofy and friendly guy
This guy that's always laid back
So laid back that he isn't going with the flow at all.
So laid back he IS the flow.
But wait a minute!
I'm having a bad day actually.
Some shit has been piling up on me...
and I'm...
Oh, sorry. Never mind.
I forgot I've got this idea to live up to...
But I've got a situation
I'm in this fight here
It's me against Matt
I guess you could say it's a fight for my life.
A fight that needed to happen ages ago.
(I swear I heard the round 1 bell)
See, I am all of those good things.
That's not even a choice.
Just who I am.
Like a twofer, the rest comes with that though.
I can be down
I can be hurt
I can...
Surprised?
Aren't you?
Guess what though?
I'm not always going to be OK.
Not always going to be good with giving and giving

Giving with no acknowledgement
No seeing that I can have a shitty day too
That when that happens, I might not be happy about it.
That when the shit hits the fan,
When my day is rocked,
That it might carry the same weight as a good day.
That it might even be heavier.
I feel everything.
Honestly, sincerely, wholly.
As.
I.
Should.
It's tricky, some don't want to believe that.
Because when they do, it's accepting I may need help too.
And God fucking forbid another person is part of why I hurt.
It's duel punishment for that.
How dare I be upset or hurt by that?
"Until you feel better, I'll lay low Matt."
Thanks.
I had no interest in solving shit anyway.
Don't worry, the happy goof will move on.
Sorta.
Because I forgive so quickly.
Forgetting never.
Even when details can't be remembered,
My heart keeps the tab.
Right there is where my reasons live.
The brick layers.
The architects.
The wall gets built there.
No matter how out going.
How friendly.
How caring.
How loving.
How giving.
How warm I am.
These bricks are thick.
So fucking thick.
So fucking thick I can't see doors or windows.
They're in there though.

The way is through some Temple of Doom,
Booby traps and all for anyone that comes in.
Myself included.
The heart beats on.
The heart beats on.
I know these walls aren't forever.
I know they aren't.
I hope...
I also know how I'm seen -
Goofy, kind, smart, laid back, sensitive, giving, loving...
I know what I hide -
Anxiety, sadness, hurt, scarring, dents, damage, insecurities...
Who I am is not a choice.
I'm everything everyone sees me as.
And everything unseen too.
This is who I am.
If I'm up.
If I'm down.
There's a ton to have.
Tons more to learn.
Tons more to learn.
This is who I am.

At the Bar

I've tried hard to
I've tried hard not to
A fact about me, a fact about how I do -
If I saw you across a bar -
I wouldn't talk to you
Not because I'm some snob
Or because a snob is how I'd describe you
Both are nowhere near the truth
But because I don't want you thinking I do what the rest of them do
I'm afraid you'd think that
And honestly, I wouldn't blame you if you did
Missing bravery is why you won't hear from me
Deficiency in courage to prove to you that there's the others,
Then there's me.
Even if they use the same words,
My version is said with sincerity.
So instead, I sit on my side of the bar
In my head, the perfect conversation plays itself out
We smile at what the other says
Laugh at the jokes cracked
All over a few drinks we get in that zone
That zone where the rest of the bar fades away
No peripheral except an occasional refocus for refills.
The night winds into the earliest of the next day
We close the bar.
I walk you to your car
Our conversation doesn't stay back in the bar
Smiles, and laughs, and connections made
You tell me this is something you almost never do
I tell you that too
And we both know what we just said is true
You search for a pen,
And finding it,
You write your number on a random receipt
I do the same and it's an even trade
And before we say goodnight, we kiss
A short kiss,
But the reaction it causes

All the buzzing and warmth of a beehive
We both take quick breaths that turn into grins,
Grins that glow and radiate
You squeeze my hand.
Then we go our own ways,
But we'll see each other again soon,
So the grins turn into smiles and stay.
Though that's the play in my head
So I finish my beer and pay my tab
And leave a tip for my bartender instead.
That night stays as a waking dream,
As does the chance to say:
"I don't want to hear I'm not like the others.
I want to hear there's no one quite like me."

Meghan

Now I'm not trying to unravel the mysteries of the universe,
I wouldn't, even if I could
But I'm telling you,
I can hear it sometimes.
From the little to the grand
It's all there.
Like this one time I used a hashtag,
Just a simple phrase
A simple glance to see who else said what
It was then that this door opened
And there was this light there.
You better believe I did
I know you know I did
Since then, we've seen wavelengths
We've surfed them
And the surf is good.
So good
It's as easy to see as anything,
Some bad news and vibes want control?
Nope
Your messages come to clear the air
Bad moods don't have a chance
But the unraveling of the mysteries of the universe?
I'll leave that to some greater poets,
Maybe even a physicist.
Wavelengths
Like when I see some news about a singer you like,
So I tell you,
And you're already listening to her?
Yeah, wavelengths.
Or that in my days I see lots of money
(most of which isn't mine)
Now, I'm not saying I know how,
But guess what I see?
Not the answers to the mysteries cosmic.
I see a lot of New York quarters.
Or these other times I'm making change into dollars and the only two quarters left were Vermont

And yes...
New York.
I can't say that I know even a fraction of everything.
But, I do know about World Poetry Day,
Hashtags,
Hockey,
The frustrations and triumphs of technology,
The Triumphs of technology,
The teams that win and win,
The blinking ellipsis,
And the smiles made.
As for the universe...
I don't have any answers for that.
Instead, I have this poem.
And now, so do you.

Going Home (November 3, 2012)

There has always been a magnetism about it.
Like a migrating bird that just knows where to go.
It's as natural as that.
Without any doubt.
This trip was different though.
A pull stronger than gravity itself,
So I didn't fight it.
Why would I?
Stepping on to the Orange Line I knew right where I was going.
I woke up that morning with a driven spirit.
There was no other thought (as if there was any chance of that).
I was going home to where my soul took human form.
I switched to the Red Line, my heart getting heavier by the stop,
Sitting on the train, I carried a cargo that weighed tons.
Damn heavy. Getting heavier and heavier. Not sure I was breathing.
The train pulls into my stop, my street, my grounds.
As I stepped, I felt what I haven't in a long, long time.
I prayed. For what, I'm still not sure.
The crisp November air fills my lungs, I'm here.
I feel that Dorchester air, sun, breeze, the son came home.
Seeing the sign for Samoset, my street, hits me like a brick to the face
My chest, I could've sworn it was being crushed.
I see that sign, and I cry the tears of the most mixed emotions I have ever felt.
They say homecomings can be hefty, and they also say shit can get real.
I'm standing at the corner of Samoset and Centre
Just reading that sign I can sensed myself sinking
Sinking into the sidewalk like it's some sort of urban quicksand
There was no motion in my body but deep breathing and tears.
Dorchester, a native son in his native land.
I walked the streets of my childhood.
Every step was more familiar than the last.
It all came back. Every thought, every memory.
I was back home and there is no doubt about that.
I was baptized here.
I spoke to God for the first time here.
I started who I am and who I will be here.
I was home again, so I kept walking because I was.

Seeing places my mind's eye always let me see and never let me forget,
The feeling like I never left and I had been away too long at the same time,
The perfect intersection of then, now, and later.
Walking onto Dot Ave., even more surged back.
That's the store my parents bought cigarettes at.
The store that if I rode my bike past, I'd go further than Ma wanted me to.
Of course I went further.
This time I turned left.
The left took me to the front Saint Mark's.
I made my way to Our Lady of the Streets.
As a son, I thanked her for delivering the world her Son.
Her Son is who I found next when I looked for something else.
I was looking for the tree Stacey kissed me and said we'd get married under,
Instead I found Him standing there like He knew I was coming.
All I could do is ask Him to help me keep asking the right questions.
As warm tears flowed I knew I'd be alright.
When that happens, when I'll be alright, I didn't know, but I knew that I would.
For nothing else other than that's just what I do.
That's always the way I've done it, I won't ever stop. (He reminded me)
I slowly made my way back to the train.
I stopped at the corner of my old school,
The corner I was sent to when I "questioned the sisters too much."
The dust of discipline's chalk was still there.
I wondered if those kids asked too many questions too.
I smiled as my imagination gave me a menagerie of possibilities.
"I feel what you're going through kids. I'm fine. And you will be too.
I'm was and am that work in progress, you are and you'll be too. Don't stop asking."
As trips home can do, so much was confirmed.
My yearning for answers will never be stagnant.
But so much more than answers is what I want,
I want my curiosity intact so I can keep looking for and asking the right questions.

Wordfare

Isn't it funny that what is said,
And what is meant,
Could not be further apart from each other?
That sometimes intent changes all meaning?
Even if that's unbeknownst to who it's said to.
Or who said it.
It's almost like we all speak in some code,
A code in which words change meaning depending on who says them,
Or who hears them,
Or some live and hyperactive combination of the two.
Words.
Long and short.
Either easy or difficult to pronounce.
Words.
We all depend on them,
We all have been known to hang on them,
Leaving us prone to hang *by* them.
That knot can be tight.
Too tight and tighter for differing definitions.
Proof -
Loyalty that can be seen in bullet holes from taking shots for others,
But showing that doesn't mean it's money in the bank,
A savings protecting us from blade shaped scars between the shoulders.
There's word misuse and abuse too…
"Love" is a common victim to this.
People carelessly using that word as if it's synonymous with "enjoy" or "like."
(Though I know those that use it carefully and truthfully)
Or telling someone in a way that can only be heard as true and honest,
But, heartbreakingly, isn't.
Love from the wrong mouth to the right heart.
Or is it right mouth, wrong heart?
Either way, damaging.
Falling in love.
Said that way because even with perfect air currents under the wings,
It hurts like hell to land wrong.
Words.
Beautiful/Ugly
Tepid/Aggressive

Kind/Hurtful
Pleasurable/Painful
Caring/Callow
Singular meaning/Multiple meanings
To "who really knows the meaning?'
Words.
Leaving everyone of us in one of two states:
In the know.
Or in confusion.
All determined by intent,
the tone,
the choices of the users.
Why else would "soon" mean "wait longer still?"
"Sometime" mean "probably never?"
"Someone" mean "no one?"
That when a person speaks of "other fish,"
The "great big sea" still looks so empty?
We've all heard these words before.
We've all said these words before.
We all know these words by heart.
So, you really don't have to take my word for it, do you?

Race Day (Hopeless Romantic or Romantic Hopeless)

(It's safer on the inside.)
Heart lives on the outside.
My heartbeat is my compass, making it too easy to lose track,
But Heart brings me back.
Fact.
Heart filters my view of the world,
But, lately Heart's got me writing poems about girls.
Heart's got his own logic,
His own way. Brain can't use it, he'd look sick.
Maybe that's why Mouth always sounds like *he's* got nothing to say.
Leaving nothing to black and white, only variants of gray.
Thought I drank the sweetest of juices.
Should've known it was all fittings for all of the tightest nooses.
With every sip I should've had at least a sliver of a hunch
That what I had been drinking was spiked punch.
She has a boyfriend who's name isn't mine.
No action attached to when she said I'm "one of a kind."
I suppose her means justify her ends
When the only way we'll ever be described is "just friends."
Which is all good.
Which is all fine.
Which is all fair.
But, man, she didn't stop there.
"You're the nicest guy," she said. "You'll definitely be a hit!"
But, I'm still on some 'nice guys finish last' shit.
I'd like to say I'm so far behind I think I'm in first place.
Though the truth is, I'm probably not even in the race.
Missed the gun. I'm still in the blocks.
Shyness or insecurity or whatever holding me down like a sack of rocks.
Like "swimmin' with the fishes."
Drowning in the depths of wishes.
(Drowning in wishes, I stay a hopeless romantic, or romantic hopeless, in the deepness of wishes.)

Hip Hop (In The Name of Love)

My kicks on the concrete
Sun in my face
The track hits my ears, electrifies my mind, moves my feet
Takes my heart back to that place
Hip Hop
Hip Hop was my genesis
I'm that little kid on a Red Line train,
Looking out windows at art so vibrant it can't be blurred or dulled by rain
All that done with paint from a can
Damn, never doubt a man with a plan
Walking by the playgrounds, I can hear a beat
I get closer and see people dancing with more than just their feet
Flattened out cardboard boxes as a makeshift dance floor
I couldn't get enough, I would always want to see more
It was then my ears started to hear
Beats that made my head nod and wordplay bombardiers
I was soaking in the five elements of Hip Hop
It's like that, and it didn't stop
Hip Hop would give me my voice,
Showed me poetry and made words my weapons of choice
My entire world opened up because of dance, beats, and rhymes
Art on trains, trailers, and walls finished the design
My world is still expanding and thankfully with no end
I hope I did this shout out "Hip Hop Hooray" style and not miss one friend
A tribute to what energizes me
Honoring what moves me
Sending peace to what powers me
Love to what empowers me
Microphone Fiends
Blast Masters
Hard Rhymers
Abstract Poets
Donuts
Wonders
I'm here now
From the dopest beat
To the Adidas on my feet
From the bottom to the top I can't stop, won't stop
I love you Hip Hop

Waking Up

I woke up this morning feeling mortal again,
Knowing that someday my heartbeat will stop,
That my days here will end.
With that quick and lightning flash,
It's not always just that life is too short,
though to many it really is,
It's that life is fast.
As all of this floods my thoughts.
Grabs my heart.
Wets my eyes.
I woke up this morning feeling mortal again.
Reminders came to make sure I felt it.
That weight of those that came into my life and left marks.
And those that left before me.
All at once I remember the ones that aren't here anymore.
At the same time I wonder about my own departure.
Echoes of "the good die young,"
Coupled with others tagging me as a "good guy."
Am I on borrowed time?
If so, when do I pay that loan back?
But, I always think of who I've met.
Everyone not here.
Definitely everyone still here.
I think of it like I don't have friends,
Instead, I have family.
Believe that if I've called you friend that name is meant for a lifetime. (And more.)
It's up to us to keep it.
To make it.
To keep it strong.
To get it to grow.
Or if paths differ,
Learn.
I woke up this morning feeling mortal again.
Though not in a way that makes me afraid to die.
Instead, in a way that makes me feel this:
When I reach my end, whenever that is, I can look back and firmly and sincerely and lovingly say that I was never afraid to live and to love.

Dedicated to YOU: my friends, my family.

A Very Special Thanks To My Kickstarter Backers

Shauna
Lydia D.
Sarah R.
Kelsey
Albie
Chris W.
Chris G.
Christa
Sarah J.
Paul D.
Sean
Jeremy
Drew
Jaime
Maria
Lydia K.
Jenn
Julie
Kerri
Nicole
Chris O.
Peter
Jennifer
Cris
Tommy
Linda
Kevin C.
Ben
Davie
Davis
Alexandria Funk
Jeff
Kevin M.
Catherine
Terri

To Coconuts (An Anti-Ode) *Hidden Track* ☺

Your appearance is a precursor to your awful taste
All brown and hairy and tough
The effort to open you is never worth the "reward"
(Don't get me started on your texture)
Why you exist is beyond my thinking
The Devil's droppings is what you are!

About the Poet

By way of Massachusetts, New Hampshire, and Vermont, Matthew is a born and raised New Englander. Born in Boston (Dorchester), he now resides in White River Junction, Vermont. Poetry has been a long time passion and this little book here a long time dream.

Between writing poems Matthew has worked with youth of various ages, including teaching high school English. Poet, audiophile, bookworm, this is Matthew's first collection of poetry.

www.ingramcontent.com/pod-product-compliance
Lightning Source LLC
Chambersburg PA
CBHW072036060426
42449CB00010BA/2286